Discarded Ancestors

At the Intersection of Art and Ancestry

Elizabeth Leader

A City of Light Imprint

A City of Light Imprint

City of Light Publishing
266 Elmwood Avenue, #407
Buffalo, NY 14222
www.CityofLightPublishing.com

Book design by Goulah Design Group, Inc.

ISBN: 978-1-942483-73-1 (softcover)
ISBN: 978-1-942483-74-8 (hardcover)

Library of Congress control number available upon request.

Printed in South Korea

10 9 8 7 6 5 4 3 2 1

Discarded Ancestors

Elizabeth Leader

About the Cover

Discarded photos and abandoned buildings covered with graffiti
are easy to find in Buffalo, New York, and throughout the Rust Belt.
But what some people pass off as mere urban decay, mixed media
artist Elizabeth Leader sees as the raw material of stories about our
past and our future. She explores these fascinating layers of time in
the collage, *The House of Little Cakes*.

Contents

To the millions of people, many of them immigrants and refugees, who worked to build up the great industrial heartland of America, that wide swath around the Great Lakes, from Chicago to Detroit to Cleveland and to Buffalo and beyond. To all the people who lived through the area's decline as it came to be scorned as the "Rust Belt." To all the people living here now who are rediscovering its value and creating a renaissance.

ELIZABETH LEADER

Preface

How This Journey Began

While walking one day on the East Side of Buffalo, New York, I found a photo album tossed to the curb in front of a decaying house. Apparently, there was no one left to care for these legacies, so like so many, they became discarded ancestors.

The photos seemed so precious; I wanted to preserve them in some form. Each picture was unique and yet so universal that it could be of almost anyone's family. I took a group of the photos out of the album and surrounded them with bits and pieces of graffiti, old paper and wood, and then layered all this over photographs I had been taking of abandoned houses and shuttered factories. I had not grown up in the area and didn't know its history, yet right in front of my eyes was prima facie proof of a glorious past and a tragic decline. What had happened here?

These collages are my attempt to bring the past and present together and to honor these people. I hope their spirits are happy being part of my art rather than discarded as trash.

Eleanor

Foreword

Discovering Eleanor

In 2016, there was an exhibit of a small collection of Elizabeth Leader's "Discarded Ancestors" collages in the Peter A. and Mary Lou Vogt Gallery at Andrew L. Bouwhuis Library at Canisius College in Buffalo, New York.

I have a great interest in genealogy and the photos intrigued me. I offered to track down the original owners of the photo album. I found the name "Eleanor" written on the backs of several of the photos. The surname "Weinzierl" was on a Fotomat envelope containing negatives that had been tucked into the album. Some of the negatives corresponded to photos in the album.

Armed with the surname Weinzierl, I went searching for an obituary. I located a 2011 obituary for an Eleanor Weinzierl in *The Buffalo News*. Then, through the "Find a Grave" site, I discovered that Eleanor and her parents were buried in Mount Calvary Cemetery in Cheektowaga, a suburb of Buffalo. She had no siblings and no children, so although she was survived by some cousins, there was no one left to keep her family photos. They were discarded, just waiting for Elizabeth to find them.

Eleanor's story spoke to me. To me, "lost" ancestors are those who have few or no direct descendants to remember them, whose stories die with them. I have some "lost" ancestors in my family but I try my hardest to learn and preserve their stories.

Eleanor's discarded photos also inspired me to look for her story because I know that some of my own family photos were lost. I only wish that somebody like Elizabeth had been there to find them.

LISA M. SULLIVAN
Librarian, Canisius College and amateur genealogist

Weinzierl Family Timeline

1912 Frank immigrates to the United States at 24 years of age. He travels on the USS Pennsylvania from Hamburg, Germany to New York, NY.

1925 Crescentia Immigrates to the United States traveling on the S.S. Orduna, coming through Ellis Island.

1927 Crescentia gives birth to a daughter, Eleanor, on April 18.

1930 Census Report: Frank is a 42-year-old single border living at 80 Zenner Street #55, in Buffalo, NY.

No school, not a veteran.

Able to read and write.

Working as a baker.

Frank and Crescentia are married on July 8. Crescentia becomes a housewife.

1935 The Weinzierl family lives at 215 Fourgeron Street, Buffalo, NY (*now a parking lot*).

Frank is employed as a cooper at the George F. Stein Brewery (*George F. Stein Brewery opened in 1935 on Broadway Avenue; it closed in 1958*).

1941 Frank is employed at Downs Brewery (*Downs opened in 1939 and closed in 1947*).

1888 Frank Paul Weinzierl is born on October 12, in Munich, Germany.

1915 Frank works as a stableman at 1605 Genesee Street.

1926 Frank is employed as a baker, living at 247 Box Avenue.

1942 Crescentia is naturalized on October 5 in the U.S. District Court of Western New York.

1888

1895 Crescentia M. Hausmann is born in Germany.

1917 Frank files a WWI Draft Registration Card (*notes he had served two years as a private in the German Infantry*).

He is described as Caucasian, short with a medium build, brown hair, and grey eyes.

He is single.

He works as a laborer at the Lumen Bearing Company on Lathrop Street (*it opened in 1900, and closed in 1963*).

1929 Various baby photos show Eleanor playing at Humbolt Park.

1930 Census Report: Dino at 4.

Dino lives with his family on Busti Avenue.

He has two brothers: Samuel, 6-years-old and George, 1-year-old.

1926 Dino Maira is born in Buffalo, NY to Italian immigrants, Joseph, 35 and Inez, 23.

1939 Eleanor completes 5th grade at 12 years of age.

1938 Eleanor makes her First Holy Communion at 11 years of age.

1950 Frank dies on January 21 at 62 years of age.

He is buried at Mt. Calvary Cemetery in Cheektowaga.

Crescentia is widowed, begins working for Goodwill Industries.

1951
Eleanor marries Dino Maira on October 20.
They live at 41 Marshall Street with Crescentia.

1959
Dino is a factory worker at Hewitt Rubber Company.

The George Stein Brewery is demolished.

1966
Eleanor is employed as a nurse's aide at St. Francis Hospital.
Dino works as a caretaker at the Buffalo & Erie County Public Library.

1969
Crescentia retires from Goodwill.

1985
Dino is employed by Erie County and lives at 296 Parkdale Avenue.
Eleanor is still employed as a nurse's aide at St. Francis Hospital which later becomes the St. Francis Nursing Home.

2012
The Lumen Bearing Company is demolished.
Eleanor's property is sold and emptied out. Furniture is tossed to the curb along with her photo album. Leader finds the album before the next trash pickup and begins the *Discarded Ancestor* series.

2018
St. Francis has become the Community Health Center of Buffalo.

2018

1951
Dino works at the Hewitt-Robins Company.

1952
Eleanor is employed as a bagger at Loblaw's.

1961
Dino is living with Eleanor at 284 Fargo Street (*now a parking lot at D'Youville College*).

1964
Dino separates from Eleanor and moves to 183 Congress Street.
Crescentia and Eleanor live together at 220 Jersey Street.

1971
Dino works as a laborer for the Department of Public Works, Buildings and Grounds.

1974
After the death of her mother, Eleanor lives at 21 Marigold Avenue.
Hewitt-Robins Industrial Rubber Co. is liquidated by Litton Industries.
Hewitt Rubber closes.

Crescentia dies on May 15 and is buried at Mt. Calvary Cemetery in Cheektowaga.

2011
Eleanor dies on January 11 at the age of 84 and is buried at Mt. Calvary Cemetery in Cheektowaga.

Her obituary mentions that she had no children but that she had cousins at the time of her death.
Eleanor was known for her great love of animals.
(*Frisky*)

2014
After remaining a vacant lot for years, 220 Jersey becomes the Mulbery Garden, part of the Fargo Estate Neighborhood Community Garden.

2016
Eleanor's identity is discovered by Lisa Sullivan based on the name Weinzierl written on a Fotomat envelope.

Growing Up

It's a mysterious world of delights and dangers, alone but better with a friend. The uniform for a little girl is a dress to the knees, white socks and Mary Jane shoes. For the boys, little black boots. Special treats are a teddy bear, a ride on a pony or sitting on the running board.

HOLD STILL! Dad is taking a photograph. Suddenly the back is straight and a look of anxiety passes over the little face.

As children grow up, the costumes appear, symbols of the church or society. So much to learn to fit into the grown-up world.

Two-year-old Eleanor at Humboldt Park Wading Pool

Girls in Bows

The House of Little Cakes

Little Black Boots

On the Running Board

Teddy

Within the image, the following text appears:

Eclairs, 483.
Chocolate, 483.
Egg Appetizer, 315
Apples, (Salad), 2
and Anchovy Can
and Sardellen App
and Sardine Sandy
and Tomato Appe
Balls, 115.
Barley

Hasen Pfeffer—Lay the rabbit meat in a jar and cover with vinegar and water, equal parts; add one sliced onion, salt, pepper, cloves and bay leaves. Allow this to soak two days. Remove the meat and brown it thoroughly in hot butter, turning it often, and gradually add the sauce in which it was pickled, as much as is required. Let simmer about a half hour or until tender.

Hasen Pfeffer

Riding on Chandler

Chocolate Fudge

Dodge St. Catholic Orphan Asylum

Queen of Trifles

Women's Lives

The Maiden is young, beautiful, unencumbered. She finds delight in a beautiful dress or a bathing suit. She faces the camera—the world—with confidence. Flirtatious, even sultry, she attracts the gaze of men. What will the future hold?

The Mother is full of joy, yet bears enormous responsibility. Will the father of her baby marry her? Will she be protected and supported? Her options are limited.

The Crone is past her child-bearing years. She is more secure, wiser. If she's a widow, she may work outside her home, provide support and guidance for her family, church and community.

Eleanor at the age of 20 in 1947

The Piano

You Don't Even Know

Pink Window

Ford Coupe

The Plaid Dress

In her White Hat

Friends

Up for Auction

Sledding

Southern Tier

Mother and Child

A Very Good Dog

The World of Men

It's a world of war and industry. The country is
screaming for soldiers and workers. A man who
survives the former can come home to the latter.
He can bake bread, brew beer, forge steel.

Men and machinery. Engines running and
smokestacks belching, creating a blanket of
industry over the city.

Pride and camaraderie shine, whether at the factory
or dressed up on a day off. But years pass quickly,
jobs move elsewhere, and factories shut down.

Metal corrodes into rust. Large, looming buildings
are demolished. Eventually only a vacant lot or
a ragged plot of grass marks the spot where they
once proudly stood.

Eleanor with her father, Frank Weinzierl

Harrison Radiator

Smoking

Chandler Street

On Their Day Off

A Gentleman

Cargill

WOOD WORKING AND
MACHINERY
was on foot, in uniform, wearing his sword, and was ac-
ompanied by one second. We advanced to meet him. He
approached holding his cap filled with black cherries. The
seconds measured twelve paces for us. I had to fire first, but
my agitation was so great, that I could not depend upon the

After the War

Soldiers

Father and Son

Tracht

Family Life

How did they manage? All of these immigrants leaving the place of their birth, traveling across the ocean to find a new life. What kept them going?

Did it help to be clustered in neighborhoods, each with its church and its taverns? The Italians, the Germans, the Poles—each ethnic group found its place within the city and could hang on to its own traditions.

Yet in this new land, it was possible for the descendents of one culture to put aside some of the old ways and be attracted to someone of a different background. A new culture was brewing in the American melting pot.

Eleanor's wedding, 1951

Parker House Rolls

After another drink, Neal insisted on a tour of the house, so I showed him the three bedrooms, parlor, and two bathrooms upstairs, and let him look at the dusty third floor I hadn't been able to furnish. He followed me down the twisting stairway to the basement, to see the air-conditioned and thumped back up to

Bridal Couple

Wedding Party

Sheriff Carl Meyer's Picnic

The Green House

The Drinking Party

Bethlehem Steel

To Bake and Stew

Fantastic Four

Epilogue

The project is complete. My remaining scraps of paper, photos and MDF board have been stored away along with the glue and paint.

The collages are out in the world carrying their traces of loss, memory and shared humanity.

Many of the houses and factories that appear as backgrounds have now been completely demolished.

There are signs of a "Rust Belt renaissance," as long vacant buildings are transformed into apartments, hotels, restaurants and new businesses.

We now look up and forward as well as back.

Acknowledgments

This journey began in solitude but over time it has drawn in many other people. I am so grateful to them all.

First, thank you to the Weinzierl and Mario families, past and present, wherever and however your family radiates out in the world.

Thank you to the people who cleaned out Eleanor's house and left the album for me to find on Marigold Street so that I could begin this journey.

Special thanks to Maria Pabico LaRotonda who invited me to display some of the collages in the Peter A. and Mary Lou Vogt Art Gallery at Canisius College, bringing this work into public view.

Thank you to Lisa Sullivan, librarian at the Andrew L. Bouwhuis Library at Canisius College whose curiosity led to the discovery of Eleanor Weinzierl's identity and the first round of information about her.

Thank you to Natalia Salansky, genealogy expert, who dove even deeper into the Weinzerl family heritage and discovered many missing pieces of the story.

Thank you to all the people who purchased the collages, thereby "adopting" the Weinzerl family. Special thanks to my husband, Harold Leader, and to Sharon Osgood and Mark Goldman for their encouragement and support.

And, special thanks to the people who helped bring this book to life: Kevin Doherty for editing, Linda Prinzi for book design, and Marti Gorman and City of Light Publishing for enthusiastically taking it on.

About the Artist

Born in Boston, Massachusetts, Elizabeth received her BFA degree at Massachusetts College of Art. She moved to Western New York to attend the Rochester Institute of Technology. After earning her MFA degree, she happily settled in Buffalo, New York, working as an art instructor and graphic designer. She has delighted in the discovery of much about her own family history as she has worked on the Discarded Ancestors series and continues her personal exploration. "We're all interconnected."

Elizabeth has exhibited her art along the East Coast, through the Rust Belt, and as far west as Alaska and Hawaii. Portions of her work have traveled around the country with the Smithonian's "Gyre" exhibition. Her work is in the permanent collection of the Everson Museum in Syracuse, at the Roswell Park Cancer Institute in Buffalo and the Aquarium of Niagara Falls, among other locations, as well as in private collections throughout the United States and internationally. Her work is also visible online at *www.elizabethleader.com*.